4    12    7

2

1

9    3

8

10

6    5    11

1  CHRISTMAS PUDDING a pudding aflame with brandy.

2  CONTEMPLATION three men in thought.

3  CONVERSATION two girls sitting on a rug by the fire.

4  CRICKET a batsman about to be caught at the wicket.

5  DANCE a girl dancing the Charleston.

6  FOOTBALL one footballer tackling another.

7  HUNTING a huntsman with his horse and dogs.

8  MUD PIE three mud pies, one with a flower stuck in the top, a pot and trowel.

9  PROFANE LOVE an embracing couple admiring themselves in a mirror, while another girl smokes a cigarette and cuddles a lapdog.

10 REST a girl reclining with a newspaper on the grass while another swings in a hammock.

11 SEA HORSE a girl playing on an inflatable horse in the sea.

12 SPEED a girl riding pillion on a motorcycle.

'Astronomy' from *The Labours of Life*, 1928

# Boris Anrep

## THE NATIONAL GALLERY MOSAICS

### LOIS OLIVER

NATIONAL GALLERY COMPANY, LONDON
DISTRIBUTED BY YALE UNIVERSITY PRESS

Acknowledgements
The author wishes to thank all those who have assisted in the preparation
of this book: Julie Adams, Benjamin Anrep, Anna Benn, Heather Birchall,
the late Annabel Farjeon, Mary Guyatt, Anne Harvey, Olivia Isherwood,
Susan Lambert, Aidan Oliver, Randi Parry, Janet Skidmore, Frances Spalding,
the staff of the Victoria and Albert Museum Print Room, the Victoria and Albert
Museum Archive, the National Art Library and the Tate Archive.


Picture Credits
Front cover, back cover and flap, pages 2, 6, 59, 62 and figs 8–24, 26–31, 33–41, 44–47
© Boris Anrep Family Estate, UK (Photo: National Gallery, London)
Figs 1, 6 © V&A Images\V&A Museum, London
Fig. 2 © Estate of Henry Lamb, London (Photo: Museum of Fine Arts, Boston)
Fig. 3 © Boris Anrep Family Estate, UK (Photo: Birmingham Museums and Art Gallery )
Figs 4,7, 48 © Boris Anrep Family Estate, UK (Photo: Courtesy of the Boris Anrep Family Estate, UK)
Fig. 5 © ADAGP, Paris and DACS, London 2004 (Photo: Tate, London)
Figs 25, 43 © Boris Anrep Family Estate, UK (Photo: V&A Images\V&A Museum, London)
Fig. 32 © The Illustrated London News, London (Photo: By Permission of The British Library, London)
Fig. 42 © By Courtesy of Cecil Beaton's Studio Archive, Sotheby's, London

Front Cover: Detail of 'Art' from *The Labours of Life*, 1928
Back Cover: Detail of 'Christmas Pudding' from *The Pleasures of Life*, 1929
Inside Flap: Detail of 'Folly' from *The Modern Virtues*, 1952

First published in Great Britain in 2004 by
National Gallery Company Limited
St Vincent House, 30 Orange Street,
London WC2H 7HH
www.nationalgallery.co.uk
*Supporting the National Gallery*

ISBN 1 85709 330 5
525323

British Library Cataloguing-in-Publication Data
A catalogue record is available from the British Library

Publisher Kate Bell
Editor Jane Ace
Design Joe Ewart for Society
Picture Researcher Kim Klehmet
Production Jane Hyne and Penny Le Tissier
Printed and bound in Italy by Mondadori

## DIRECTOR'S FOREWORD

Drawn by the grand sweep of the late Victorian staircase to the galleries beyond, it is easy for visitors entering the National Gallery to miss the mosaics on the staircase landings. Those who do pause, however, are often surprised to find at their feet a teeming cast of characters including Winston Churchill, Virginia Woolf, T.S. Eliot and Greta Garbo. They might be even more surprised to spot Lewis Carroll's Alice, a girl dancing the Charleston, a Christmas pudding and some mud pies. As a snapshot of its time, this wonderfully exuberant mosaic cycle, created by the Russian artist Boris Anrep between 1926 and 1952, is as charming and evocative as it is eccentric.

A larger-than-life character, Anrep was an intimate of the Bloomsbury Group and a close friend of Augustus John and Anna Akhmatova. His exploits included deeds of derring-do in Occupied France, competing in the men's doubles at Wimbledon, and a love-life of a complexity to rival Augustus John's. As an artist he was the first to champion mosaics in a modern style, brilliantly combining Byzantine technique with contemporary subject matter: for all their playfulness, the National Gallery mosaics represent a serious and highly personal attempt to encapsulate something of both the English national character and the nature of artistic creativity.

Drawing on previously unpublished papers, Lois Oliver traces the story of Anrep's life including the often humorous tale of the mosaic commission. When the work was finally completed the National Gallery had a remarkable work of art. I hope that next time you visit the Gallery you too will pause at the top of the stairs to take a closer look. As Anrep himself once said: 'Too much art is above people's heads...'

CHARLES SAUMAREZ SMITH
Director, The National Gallery

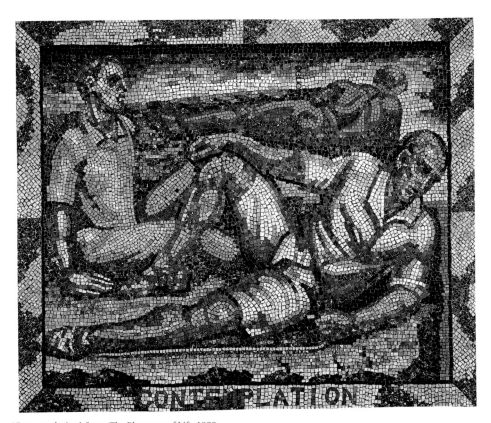

'Contemplation' from *The Pleasures of Life*, 1929

# BORIS ANREP AND THE NATIONAL GALLERY MOSAICS

*I was always interested in floors as a space eminently suitable for pictorial mosaics. It is more natural for us to look down than to look up to a decorated ceiling... the sight of pavement artists outside the National Gallery gave me the idea of decorating the floors of the vestibule. I approached the Director, Sir Charles Holmes. I had luck and the Director and the Trustees agreed. I got in on the ground floor while the other pavement artists, poor beggars, are still outside the Gallery.*

Boris Anrep [1]

1. Boris Anrep

So it was that the Russian artist Boris Anrep (fig. 1) came to create four mosaic marble floors for the National Gallery entrance hall between 1926 and 1952. This cycle of mosaics – the first works of art to greet visitors to the Gallery – demonstrates brilliantly Anrep's unique combination of Byzantine technique, modern subject matter and wit. Within the geometrical layout and leaf borders appear portraits of famous figures of the day, including such characters as Winston Churchill, Virginia Woolf and Bertrand Russell, many of whom were personally known to the artist.

## A RUSSIAN ABROAD

Boris Anrep was born on 28 September 1883 in St Petersburg, the son of a distinguished physiologist and medical administrator, Vasily von Anrep, and his wife Prascovia Zatzepina. He went to school in Kharkov and in 1899 was sent to Great Missenden, Buckinghamshire for the summer to learn English. From 1902 Anrep studied law at the prestigious Uchilishche Pravovedeniya (Legal Academy) in St Petersburg and on graduating in 1905 looked set for an academic career.

Anrep decided, however, that he wished to become a painter and poet. He mixed with the St Petersburg literary elite, and took painting lessons with the artist Dimitri Stelletsky. Inspired by Stelletsky, he travelled widely in Russia, the Near East, Greece and Italy, developing a passion for Russian icons and Byzantine art. He was particularly enthralled by examples of ancient Roman mosaics and by the dazzling sixth-century Byzantine mosaics at Ravenna in northern Italy. He later said this had inspired him to work in mosaic.

In 1908 he married Yuniya Kitrovo and the couple moved to Paris so that Anrep could continue his studies in art. He enrolled at the Académie Julian and over the next few years also worked in various ateliers and mosaic factories. He spent the winter of 1910–11 at Edinburgh College of Art and began making regular visits to London. A fellow student at the Académie Julian was Henry Lamb, who introduced him to the artist Augustus John and his wife Dorelia, and to the Bloomsbury circle, including the writer Lytton Strachey, the economist John Maynard Keynes and the celebrated hostess Lady Ottoline Morrell. They were very taken with the foreigner, whom Lady Ottoline described as: 'clever, fat, good-hearted, sensual, but full of youthful vitality and Russian gaiety.'[2] She introduced Anrep to Roger Fry, and in 1912 Anrep selected the Russian exhibits for Fry's Second Post-Impressionist exhibition in London, bringing artists such as Mikhail Larionov and Natalya Goncharova to the attention of a British audience for the first time.

Yuniya also attracted attention and admiration. Lady Ottoline described her as a 'fair childlike creature, very Russian, gay and clever',[3] while Henry James observed that her 'little ringlets of pale yellow fluff looked as if they would come off with her hat'.[4] Her marriage to Anrep did not last however. In Paris Anrep had met Helen Maitland, a close friend of Dorelia John and ex-girlfriend of Henry Lamb, and although Anrep was still married to Yuniya, Helen lived with them from 1911. Helen gave birth to a daughter, Anastasia, in 1912 and a son, Igor, in 1914. Shortly afterwards Yuniya returned to Russia.

2. Henry Lamb, 1885–1960
*Boris Anrep and his Family*, about 1920
Oil on panel, 95.3 × 157.5 cm, Tompkins Collection, Museum of Fine Arts, Boston

At the outbreak of war in 1914 Anrep went to serve in the Imperial Russian Guard, fighting in Galicia until 1916. Away from Helen, he became romantically involved with the Russian poet Anna Akhmatova, to whom he had been introduced before the war by his step-brother Vladimir. Anrep described the relationship that developed as no more than a 'warm friendship' but for Akhmatova it was intensely important.[5] Given Anrep's reputation at the time (to Aldous Huxley, who met him in 1916, he was the epitome of the shameless philanderer) and Akhmatova's own Bohemian lifestyle, it seems unlikely that the relationship was entirely platonic.[6] Akhmatova's love for Anrep inspired over thirty poems, which trace the passage of their affair from her early hopes and dreams to her bitter disappointment at their parting.

In 1917 Anrep was called back to London as Military Secretary to the Russian Government Committee, setting sail for Aberdeen in April. In his care on the ship was the eighteen-year-old Mariya Volkova (known as Maroussia), the sister of Anrep's brother Gleb's wife, Olga. Maroussia had been offered employment as a typist by the Russian Government Committee. During the journey they began an affair. When Anrep divorced Yuniya and married Helen in 1918 he invited Maroussia to live with them at 4 Pond Street, Hampstead. She can be seen sorting tesserae in the background of Henry Lamb's family portrait of Anrep with Helen and their two children, Anastasia and Igor (fig. 2). 'Helen had learnt to accept Boris's need for two wives', wrote Frances Spalding, 'as she had learned to accept that when he went out socially in Mayfair, both wives were expected to stay at home.' As Spalding noted, it was the birth of Igor that had prompted Anrep to marry Helen. 'Had the child been a daughter their unmarried state would have continued, but Boris disapproved of illegitimate sons. "There's no sense in marriage," he once said. "I prefer collages – associations that everyone knows about."'[7] Nevertheless, Anrep caused jealous scenes when Helen, fed up with the *ménage à trois*, left him in 1926 to live with Roger Fry.

Anrep was an attractive man 'of near Herculean size and shape',[8] who was 'reputed to be the only man in London capable of standing up to Augustus [John] in a fist fight'.[9] He was a keen tennis player (competing in the men's doubles at Wimbledon in 1920), an excellent cook (particularly famed for his mayonnaise recipe) and a generous and hospitable host who delighted in the company of his friends. Frances Partridge's most vivid memory of him was 'in the house at Hampstead where he lived with Helen and his children, genially presiding over a table groaning with specially cured hams and deliciously dressed salads'. She remembered that 'as a guest he was equally generous, often arriving with a lavish supply of smoked salmon, and once with a wonderfully rich Russian Easter cake, decorated with crystallised fruit and spiked like a hedgehog with almonds. If one protested he would say almost angrily and obviously truthfully: "But I LIKE to do it".'[10] Anrep also took trouble to send appropriate gifts to his friends and acquaintances. In the early 1920s he surprised Virginia Woolf with a photograph of Tolstoy. Thanking him, she wrote, 'you must have a particular genius for knowing people's tastes – my feeling for Tolstoy is such that an old boot-button of his would be a treasure to me (of course I should lose it very soon) but this snapshot is much better, and I shall paste it into a book and never lose it'.[11]

Although Anrep never lost his heavy Russian accent, he was a fine conversationalist, who used English with flair. 'Listening to his talk,' wrote Partridge, 'the sensitive and surprising modulations of his voice and brilliant choice of words, and watching the drift of expressions across his face, from a look of bitter scorn to a broad, sly pussy-cat smile, one was forever trying to fix some wonderful phrase in memory, only to have it ousted by another. He was infinitely curious, and liked to discuss or talk or hear, about almost anything. He was also an excellent listener, receiving gossip or information with a gratifying expression of delighted astonishment, and a long drawn out "No-o-o-o? Ree-ee-ally?" … He loved conversation and would often start an argument among his Bloomsbury friends by some provocative premise – about the futility of art galleries and museums or the importance (and the shortage) of talented and dedicated hostesses. As for his stories, one could listen to them for ever.'[12]

Augustus John was instrumental in promoting Anrep's work and in obtaining for him a number of his early commissions in England. John persuaded the art dealer Jack Knewstub to arrange an exhibition of Anrep's drawings, paintings and mosaics at the Chenil Gallery in Chelsea in October 1913, for which Fry wrote an introduction to the catalogue. In his artist's statement Anrep declared himself a passionate advocate for the art of mosaic, which he wrote, 'has been completely forgotten. By this Art men have been enabled to create supreme and eternal symbols of Christian Divinity. Now it has degenerated on the one hand into Florentine souvenirs for ladies' boudoirs, on the other into lifeless imitations of academical paintings.'[13]

In 1914 the society hostess Ethel Sands commissioned Anrep to design a mosaic floor for her entrance hall at 15 The Vale, Chelsea, which was laid in 1917 after his return from the war. She was delighted with the result, and three years later commissioned him to decorate the walls as well. Witty and light-hearted, the scheme included vignette portraits of Lytton Strachey and his companion Dora Carrington looking towards each other from cottage windows, and Virginia Woolf dressed in male costume with her head among the stars. Around them grew a mosaic garden, with trellises, roses and a statue of Venus all presented in an exuberant yet perfectly harmonious ensemble.[14]

Anrep delighted in producing particularly appropriate mosaics for his friends. A 1919 mosaic family portrait for Augustus John's Chelsea house showed John at the top of a pyramid of wives and children, while in 1921 Anrep produced a fireplace for Lytton Strachey – who had conceived a passion for the blond, burly Russian – which depicted a naked hermaphrodite, strongly resembling Carrington, swimming across the lintel and gazing seductively over an outstretched arm.

In 1922 the eminent lawyer William Jowitt and his wife Lesley commissioned a mosaic floor for their Mayfair home at 35 Upper Brook Street, showing various daily incidents in the life of a lady of fashion. Lesley Jowitt is shown telephoning from her bed dressed in pyjamas (fig. 3), in her bath, applying lipstick at her dressing table, attending an exhibition of African sculpture, at the dressmaker's, in a box at the theatre, shaking cocktails and dancing at a nightclub. For Fry, the work was a milestone: 'Here at last he is able to treat a completely modern theme, the daily life of a lady of fashion in the year 1922, in a manner which belongs to the artistic vision of today and to no other period in the history of Art, and yet – and here is his triumph – to treat it with exactly the same sense of the monumental and resistant qualities of

3. *Daily Incidents in the Life of a Lady of Fashion* (detail), 1922
Birmingham City Art Gallery

the medium as the Byzantine mosaicists displayed... Mr Anrep has shown how admirably mosaic is suited to the interior decoration of private houses and secular public buildings, and that for all the apparent inflexibility of the medium it is possible to be as witty and mischievous in the grand style of monumental design as in any other. I say as witty – I might have said more witty – for there is a peculiar piquancy in Mr Anrep's sly allusions to the more trivial details of everyday life.'[15] The public commission to which Fry alluded was the mosaic floor that Anrep completed in 1923 for the Blake Room in the Tate Gallery at Millbank, illustrating 'The Proverbs of Hell' from *The Marriage of Heaven and Hell* by William Blake.


IN THE PARIS STUDIO

After Helen left him in 1926, Anrep returned to Paris with Maroussia. He took a studio in the Latin Quarter at 65 Boulevard Arago (fig. 4), which he sublet from the painter Pierre Roy (another former student of the Académie Julian, see fig. 5) and it was there that he worked on the public commissions that he was now receiving. In 1940 he and Maroussia escaped from Paris on the day the Germans entered the city, an adventure that Anrep never tired of recounting to delighted listeners. Having secured places on a train to Nantes through their friendship with a railway official, they arrived only to find that the last train for Bordeaux had already

4. The studio in the Latin Quarter at 65 Boulevard Arago, Paris (Anrep is third from the right)

departed. Luckily a British officer provided them with a lorry and petrol, and after several dangerous days they were on the point of setting sail on a Dutch ship, when the captain ordered all four hundred passengers heading for Britain to disembark. Fortunately a British pilot then arrived with a dozen British sailors, commandeered the ship, and forced the captain to take them to Falmouth. Anrep took a house and studio at North End, Hampstead, became an air-raid warden, and between 1941 and 1943 worked nights as a monitor transcribing Russian broadcasts for Reuters.

After the war Anrep returned to his Paris studio. Justin Vulliamy, who worked as Anrep's assistant from the 1930s onwards recalled: 'Life in Boris's Paris studio was I think very much to his liking – he worked harder than he might have done in England, he played tennis, and entertained friends and visitors in the excellent small restaurants of the quarter.'[16]

Anrep was unusual in carrying out all of his work at his own studio, rather than simply preparing cartoons and then sending them to commercial companies to execute them in mosaic. Having spent time in mosaic factories, he always felt it was a pity that more of the work was not carried out by artists. He employed a team of assistants (many of them Russian refugees) in his studio but always did the most difficult parts of the work himself, especially heads and hands. The

5. Pierre Roy, 1880–1950
*Boris Anrep's Studio with a Bust of the Artist*, 1949
Oil on canvas, 65.3 × 50.1 cm, Tate

scene made a great impression on Nicholas Henderson, who was taken to visit Anrep's Paris studio as a child: 'The men humped sacks onto the trestle tables and chipped pieces of marble; while the women, ill-looking but resigned, helped in the making of the mosaics as though engaged in some giant jigsaw. Boris himself, dressed like his workers in overalls, sat on a high stool. With a Gauloise cigarette on his lower lip, a large fore-arm extended over the table, he applied himself to the more difficult parts of the work and supervised the whole team with genial authority.'[17]

Glass and gold tesserae were ordered from the famous Venetian mosaic supplier Angelo Orsini, while coloured marbles, used for floor mosaics, were sourced from a number of Italian quarries. An unpublished memoir by Vulliamy gives a vivid description of work within the studio:

Occupying most of the floor space was the big table of plywood, waist-high upon trestles: above it, as it were over a billiard table, a cluster of lampshades suspended from a cat's cradle of wires, among which dangled some ostrich eggs giving it all a sort of orthodox flavour... The table, by far the largest object in the room, served both as a store for sacks of material beneath, and on its upper surface of course as the platform upon which the mosaic work was made. As well as mosaic itself, segments of which generally remained covered when not being worked, the table held an array of apparatus, cutting machines, tools, recipients [sic] of all kinds: bottles, jars, glasses, pots of gum, paints, brushes, rolls of paper and newspapers of all kinds in several languages. Around the table's edge half a dozen stools. Any spare space around the walls was used for storage of materials, on shelves, and on the floor in boxes, bags and sacks. Anyone who ever saw the studio will remember the appearance of permanent disorder, the counterpart in reality of a fairly rigorous discipline. The nature of the work produced much debris, constantly being swept up, but in places inaccessible to the broom, there lay a dust of decades... On going into the studio, Boris took his coat off, put on a blue apron over his grey cardigan, rolled up his sleeves and took up his central place seated on his stool before the large work-table. At hand were his hammer, a pot of gum containing a small brush, a horn-handled knife, a pair of surgical forceps and if the work was of marble, a large damp sponge to wet the stones better to see their true colours, once gummed down on paper. The essential mosaic tool is the cutting hammer, Italian in origin, with a fine steel head about a hand's span long with a sharp cutting edge tempered like a chisel at each end, in the frontal plane; the mosaic tesserae are struck and trimmed upon another essential, yet to be mentioned, the metal anvil... Long practice had given Boris

6. Anrep's assistants levelling concrete in preparation for the Gallery mosaics (Tomaso Despert is on the left)

great skill with his hammer, large and heavy but light in his grip as, with a flick of the wrist he would split the stone more often than not into exactly the form required: this particular skill he was never tired of practising.[18]

In all his work Boris used an indirect or transfer method. Sometimes, as in the case of the National Gallery mosaics, preliminary cartoons were made in black and white chalk on brown paper. Full-sized colour cartoons would always follow. 'The cartoons were made on the kraft paper [strong brown parcel paper], strips of which were gummed together to form sheets occasionally as large as stage scenery, and these were hoisted up against the high side of the studio, for inspection, with a view to improvements – the full-sized cartoons being the reversed image of the design. Care had to be taken therefore that any lettering should be in looking-glass writing, right-handed figures made left-handed and so on. Then the other side of the cartoon was marked out on the table with a square grid, lettered and numbered, before cutting it out into many small sections. Sometimes a duplicate cartoon in colour would be made, for use as a full-sized model for reference. Then, upon the many small pieces,

7. Anrep making final adjustments to 'Christmas Pudding' from *The Pleasures of Life*, 1929

in the daily progress of the job, were assembled the mosaic stones, each stone stuck down with a touch of gum, according to the pattern and colour of the design on that particular fragment of the cartoon.'[19]

Once all the stones were in place, the fragments, still with the paper attached, were ready to be shipped to their destination. There, under Anrep's supervision, assistants would lay the floor. For this stage he had the expert help of Italian craftsmen, including the two Indri, (father and son) and Tomaso Despert, who fixed most of the upper floor at the National Gallery. A layer of cement had to be perfectly levelled before the mosaic was fixed in place (fig. 6). A few hours later the kraft paper and gum adhesive were washed off, leaving the pattern of tesserae exposed. Anrep might then make some final adjustments before the cement hardened (fig. 7). Finally the floor would be treated with a marble-polishing machine.

It was in his Paris studio, before and after the war, that Anrep did all of his work for the National Gallery. As he himself said, 'I live in France, and work for England'.[20]

## THE NATIONAL GALLERY MOSAICS

The society hostess and patron of the arts, Mrs Maud Russell, who paid for the fourth and final mosaic at the National Gallery, recorded in her diary that Anrep later told her with some embarrassment how Samuel Courtauld had been persuaded to finance the first three mosaic floors. Courtauld had discussed with Anrep a project to decorate a gallery at the back of his house in Berkeley Square, Mayfair, and when this came to nothing, 'being nice and kindly', he promised to back a public commission should the opportunity arise. So Anrep went straight to the National Gallery and told them he had a patron who would like to pay for floors at the National Gallery. The Director and Trustees were naturally delighted that such a project should be offered to them without the need to find funds.

> Their approval given, B[oris] went off to Sam, said the trustees were all for the scheme and that he, B, remembered Sam had told him he might come to him if he wanted a backer. Sam was quite pleased: he too said, 'Go ahead', and he too didn't bother to ask about price. The drawings were got out, the details settled and still no one [asked] what the cost would be, though it meant three floor spaces. Finally, when all was fixed up, Boris told Sam the price would be £8000 – £5000 for the two sides, £3000 for the centre. B thinks Sam was very surprised though he said little, and that he had vaguely thought the cost might be £700.[21]

This story is corroborated by a letter from Samuel Courtauld to Anrep, dated 8 August 1926: 'I hope I didn't imply that I thought your estimate of remuneration was fanciful. I only thought that for a big job a lower *rate* would be reasonable as compared with a smaller one, at least as I told you, that is usual in most forms of business… I have now heard from him [the Director of the National Gallery, Sir Charles Holmes] and he suggests that the Trustees may be satisfied with a guarantee for the two side landings and the central panel leaving the future to take care of the North landing. I think this is quite a good suggestion and if it is accepted it should reduce the first cost a great deal. Then with such other subscriptions as I expect them to raise, I think there should be no further difficulty about the guarantee.' Courtauld was nevertheless enthusiastic about the project, and in a letter to Anrep dated 10 October 1926 assured him that he had 'privately promised to back the whole scheme and see that you get paid in full', although he was not yet formally promising more than half the costs (£3587 10s) as he did not wish to deter other subscribers.[22] In fact, despite fundraising efforts, Courtauld was called upon to cover the bulk of the costs for the first three mosaics.

8. Sea Horse

## THE LABOURS OF LIFE AND THE PLEASURES OF LIFE

In October 1926 Sir Philip Sassoon (a Trustee of the National Gallery), Dugald Sutherland MacColl (one of the founders of the National Art Collections Fund) and Sir Charles Holmes formed a sub-committee to manage the project and comment on the designs. Anrep was free to choose a subject, and selected, for the West Vestibule, *The Labours of Life*, and for the East Vestibule, *The Pleasures of Life*.

9. Dance

10. Speed

Although the themes are traditional, Anrep's treatment of them was thoroughly modern, and delighted his contemporaries. 'By its durability and pungent symbolism mosaic is particularly suited to "pickle for posterity" some reflections of our time', wrote René MacColl in the magazine *The Studio*.[23] Girls with fashionably bobbed hair are shown engaged in pastimes that epitomise the roaring twenties: playing on an inflatable horse in the sea (fig. 8), dancing the Charleston (fig. 9), and riding pillion on a motorcycle (fig. 10). This particular subject, still thrillingly shocking to a 1920s audience, excited considerable comment. Arnold Whittick greatly admired the vitality of the girl's expression. 'The nearer eye, represented with much vividness, is rendered by two pieces, black and white; and in that glance back there is all the expression of things left behind at a great and somewhat hazardous speed.'[24] Journalists were more attracted by her hemline, the *Evening News* reporting that, 'Captain Anrep had to come to London for a model for her, because Parisian girls' legs are too fat and short'.[25] The *Pleasures* also include favourite 1920s sports: Cricket (fig. 11), Football (fig. 12) and Hunting (fig. 13). (Tennis had at one time also been considered – a preliminary sketch appeared in *Boris Anrep: A Loan Exhibition* at the Edward Harvane Gallery in 1973.) The *Labours* have a modern flavour too: an explorer using a cine-camera (see fig. 27) and an engineer using an electric drill (fig. 14). They also include a couple of scenes dedicated to London life: a Covent Garden porter carrying a tower of baskets (fig. 15), and a student studying the *diplodocus carnegii* in the Natural History Museum (fig. 16).

11. Cricket

12. Football

13. Hunting

14. Engineering

15. Commerce

16. Science

There are some traditional subjects, for example Art and Letters (figs 17 and 18). But while Art is represented in traditional manner by a sculptor, Letters reflects Anrep's lively approach to his subject matter. His first idea was to depict a pile of books, but on 28 January 1928 he wrote to Sir Charles: 'I have now changed my mind as it was looking rather tedious so I have now made a composition which I like and which represents a slate such as children use at school with four names of great English writers on it written in chalk as if by the hand of a pupil.' He also

17. Art

suggested that the names might be written in childish hand, with spelling mistakes. By 12 February 1928 Anrep had decided against 'introducing the pomposity of great names' such as Shakespeare or Milton, and chosen instead the titles of well-known children's books. Anrep finally settled on *Gulliver's Travels*, *Alice in Wonderland*, *Robinson Crusoe* and *Treasure Island* (the last of which was suggested by the committee to replace *Shock-Headed Peter*); the committee vetoed the idea of spelling mistakes, fearing that the joke 'might easily be misunderstood'.[26]

18. Letters

There are a number of idiosyncratic choices amongst the subjects depicted, reflecting Anrep's personal views. For example, Music (fig. 19) and Theatre (fig. 20) appear as labours, although Dance is included as a pleasure. The art critic Herbert Furst described the mosaic of Sacred Love (fig. 21) as 'a little family idyll consisting of mother, father, child and dog'.[27] Yet the womanising Anrep includes it in the *Labours* rather than the *Pleasures*. The hand-written note preserved on the back of

19. Music

20. Theatre

21. Sacred Love

22. Profane Love

the cartoon for Sacred Love in the Victoria and Albert Museum describes the subject in a mixture of English and French as 'a monk *sacre*' (a holy monk). The artist preferred the lifestyle of Profane Love where a man is shown with two women enjoying red wine and cigarettes (fig. 22).

Christmas Pudding (fig. 23) conveys Anrep's affection for his adopted country and his love of good food, while Mud Pie (fig. 24) reflects his sense of fun and his special gift

23. Christmas Pudding                  24. Mud Pie

for amusing children: the reporter for the *Evening News* recorded Anrep handing out mud pies of cement to a delighted horde of school children watching him lay the mosaics in the Gallery in November 1929. 'Captain Anrep', he wrote, 'is the apostle of frivolous floors; you tread on his works with chuckles of delight.' Yet the critic for *The Times* also saw a serious meaning behind the scheme, which he concluded 'appeals unobtrusively to the human instincts and aspirations from which all enduring art must spring'.[28]

Many of the original preparatory cartoons in black and white chalk on brown paper are in the Victoria and Albert Museum, and the National Gallery Archive and National Art Library hold the correspondence between Anrep and the committee detailing the development of the designs. In the original cartoon for Conversation one of the girls held a rag doll (figs 25 and 26); Hunting was originally a '*déjeuner de chasse*'; and the cartoon for Football shows four figures, rather than the two in the final version. Sir Charles Holmes wrote to Anrep on 10 January 1927:

> My dear Anrep,
> The committee inspected on Saturday your sketches for your mosaics illustrating 'The Labours of Life', and desired me to say how interesting they considered them to be. In three points, however, they wished to make suggestions.

25. Cartoon for the first version of 'Conversation', about 1929
Black and white chalk on brown paper
The Victoria and Albert Museum

1) They did not feel that the design of The Arts is as felicitous as those of the other panels and wondered whether you would mind trying a new design. They thought that if you could represent an artist at work on a statue you would have an opportunity of making a design more in harmony with the active spirit of the other panels. [It is not known what Anrep's original design depicted.]

2) It was suggested that in the Exploring [fig. 27], the introduction of some animal, an elephant, for example, would not only make a better balance to the corresponding panel [Farming, fig. 28], but would express the idea of travel in Asia or Africa more completely than your picturesque butterflies, which after all belong

26. Conversation

to a genera [sic] which are found at home as well as abroad.

3) Sacred Love. It was felt that the horse in the background was not quite fortunate, either in its scale or placing, and the committee was a little doubtful about the significance and attitude of the little dog.

Holmes also made suggestions for the titles of each scene, and at an early stage asked Anrep to remove a 'golf ball' motif from the borders of the medallions in the *Labours*, which he suggested might be 'liable to misinterpretation'. He told Anrep he thought it could appear 'obscene'.[29] Anrep replaced it with veining.

27. Exploring

28. Farming

29. The Awakening of the Muses

## THE AWAKENING OF THE MUSES

With his third mosaic, *The Awakening of the Muses*, Anrep linked the themes of the first two. At the crowing of the cock, Bacchus, patron of the pleasures, and Apollo, who inspires the labours, awaken the muses (fig. 29). The image was for Anrep a mythical depiction of the origins of art, as he explained in a Russian radio broadcast: 'it is by bringing together the intellectual force of Apollo and the more sensitive side of Bacchus that you create the greatest flowering of art.'[30]

C.H. Collins Baker, Keeper of the National Gallery, wrote to Anrep on 26 March 1930 informing him that the committee had given the authority for work to go ahead on the third floor, using the balance remaining from the sum promised for the three

floors in 1927, and asking the artist to let him know this met his views and wishes.[31] Anrep replied with characteristic humour and frankness on 27 March 1930: 'Thank you for your kind enquiry about my views and wishes. I shall be glad to execute the third mosaic on the "bridge" landing for the sum you mention, which is £2045 – so much for my views. I shall not object, however, if the price is doubled: so much for my wishes.'[32]

The board approved Anrep's design for the floor on 8 July 1930. Work was rather delayed, however, as Anrep had by now also taken on a commission for the Bank of England, a project that was to occupy him in several phases until 1946. Some entertaining correspondence in the National Gallery Archive chronicles the ongoing negotiations. The Director of the National Gallery, Sir Augustus Daniel, wrote to

Anrep on 21 Jan 1931: 'I am beginning to wonder when you will be coming over to begin the mosaic central panel of the vestibule.' Anrep replied the following day, 'Thank you for your letter. I regret to say, my work on the central panel has been put aside lately, for a very dull, but *hélas*, important commission, which I was forced to put in hand at once for the Bank of England. I thought that I could run it as a side show devoting any personal energy to the central panel of the N.G. but things turned out quite differently and by the nature of this work I have to spend so much time looking after my workmen, that I came to the conclusion that it will be better for me to postpone the completion of the central panel, since there is no time limit imposed upon me. I meant to write to you about it all this time, but I am so torn to bits by my semi-commercial undertaking at the B of E, that I have no time to think of my most urgent duties.' Eleven months later on 28 December 1931 the Director wrote again, 'It does require some restraint on our part to suffer willingly the delay in the completion of your mosaic… Do give me some idea, if you have a clear idea, when you are likely to be able to take up work here'. After receiving a couple more letters from Anrep apologising for the continued delay, an exasperated but amused Director wrote on 15 January 1932, 'Thank you so much for your letter. I love to receive them, they are so amusing even when they are delicately putting off the work here'. On 29 July 1932, Anrep promised to fix the floor in March 1933, and he eventually began laying it at the end of May. On 26 April 1933 he wrote, 'I have [sic] hoped to be ready for fixing in March but at the eleventh hour I have decided to introduce a number of birds and small animals into the picture to cheer up the landscape and it took some time as there are about fifty of them'.

As with the previous two mosaics, Anrep injected a traditional subject with a modern and personal flavour, this time by including portraits of his contemporaries, amongst them several members of the Bloomsbury Group and others from his circle of friends. Sir Osbert Sitwell, a great champion of new movements in the arts, presides as Apollo. The art critic Clive Bell, a central figure in the Bloomsbury Group and a renowned party host appears as Bacchus, god of wine. Reclining at his feet is his one-time lover Mrs St John Hutchinson, also a member of the Bloomsbury Group, as Erato, muse of Lyric Poetry. The novelist Virginia Woolf appears holding a quill pen as Clio, muse of History; she embraces Lady Jowitt, who as Thalia, muse of comedy, makes her second appearance in an Anrep mosaic, following her starring role in the mosaics that he had designed for her home in 1922. Terpsichore, muse of dancing, portrayed holding a squirrel in her hand and reclining beside a lyre, is a portrait of the Russian ballerina Lydia Lopokova, the wife of John Maynard Keynes: her inclusion provides a nice link between Anrep's Russian heritage and his Bloomsbury friends.

Three of the other muses are women famed for their beauty: the film star Greta Garbo appears as Melpomene, muse of tragedy, with a wreath of flowers in her hand and a theatrical mask beside her; the society beauty Lady Aberconway herself chose to be represented as Euterpe, muse of music, and wrote to Anrep that she loved to 'think of my marble immortality'.[33] The composer William Walton had dedicated his viola concerto to her in 1929. Next to her is Polyhymnia, muse of sacred song, shown feeding a bird; her features are those of the Hon. Mrs Bryan Guinness, née Diana Mitford, the most beautiful of the Mitford sisters. She would perhaps not have been included had the designs been produced after 1932. By the time the floor was laid in 1933, she had already been involved for a year in a very public affair with Sir Oswald Mosley, leader of the British Union of Fascists. In 1936 they eloped and were secretly married at the house of Goebbels, with Hitler present, and she spent the years 1940–3 interned at Holloway prison as a danger to the state.

The mosaic also includes a more private memento, a portrait of Maroussia as Urania, muse of astronomy, resting her hand on a ball decorated with stars. Anrep told Maud Russell that, Calliope, muse of heroic poetry, who is depicted stroking a white rabbit, was an 'Imaginary woman'. She thought that he might have wanted to do a portrait of someone he knew and then changed his mind.[34]

## THE MODERN VIRTUES

In February 1945 Boris Anrep informed the Director of the National Gallery, Sir Kenneth Clark, that he had found an anonymous patron (Mrs Maud Russell) who would like to pay for the fourth mosaic at the National Gallery, thus completing the scheme. A celebrated patron of the arts, Mrs Russell had sat for John Singer Sargent, Henri Matisse, William Nicholson and William Orpen, and in 1938 she and her banker husband Gilbert (d. 1942) had commissioned Rex Whistler to decorate the drawing room at their Hampshire home, Mottisfont Abbey, with *trompe l'œil* murals.

For Anrep, *The Modern Virtues* represented the completion of the 'philosophical cycle'.[35] While the first three floors illustrate the origins of art, the fourth plays with the idea of a National Gallery by representing the character traits of the English. As he wrote in the description submitted to the committee with the first designs, he had chosen qualities and states of mind that he considered important in modern life. Like *The Awakening of the Muses*, the mosaic incorporates portraits of famous people, this time including many eminent figures from public life, but as Anrep told

30. Defiance

his audience in an English radio broadcast, 'if there is any feeling of squeamishness in walking over august personages one can easily step round them'.

At the centre is Winston Churchill, as Defiance, dressed in his wartime siren suit and making the victory sign as a swastika-shaped monster threatens the British Isles (fig. 30). Curiosity (fig. 31) shows a crowned bust of the eminent physicist Lord Rutherford (1871–1937), the only figure to appear posthumously, beside a representation of the primitive apparatus that he used to split the atom. The philosopher Bertrand Russell (fig. 32) appears as Lucidity, drawing the figure of Truth from a well and plucking off her last garment, a mask (fig. 33). Anrep was no doubt delighted that Truth was traditionally represented as a naked woman, as the image was so deliciously appropriate for Russell, a man famous not only for his pursuit of philosophical truth but also for his pursuit of the ladies. (His lovers had included Lady Ottoline Morrell and T.S. Eliot's wife Vivienne.) Anrep

31. Curiosity

also included a personal tribute to Russell's philosophical detachment with regard to public honours: on a shelf behind him is a princely crown, which Anrep explained in his Russian radio broadcast represents 'the title which he never used, Sir Bertrand Russell'. Anrep himself later refused a knighthood.

Many of the subjects betray Anrep's characteristic sense of humour. The astronomer Fred Hoyle, personifying Pursuit, is depicted as a steeplejack climbing ever closer to the stars (fig. 34). Anrep had originally conceived this image as a 'reference to the exploit of a Cambridge undergraduate who climbed a

32. Bertrand Russell looking at his portrait in 'Lucidity' from *The Modern Virtues*, 1952

33. Lucidity

steeple and placed a chamber-pot on its top'.[36] Anrep's old friend William Jowitt, by now Earl Jowitt, Lord Chancellor and a Trustee of the National Gallery, appears in his Lord Chancellor's robes as Open Mind, before statues of Justice and the three-headed Janus (fig. 35). Janus symbolises the wisdom and circumspection that precedes a fair judgement, although, as Anrep told his Russian radio audience, 'malicious rumour might interpret the three-headed Janus otherwise'. Jowitt's controversial parliamentary career had seen him change political allegiance three times, most notoriously just three days after being elected

34. Pursuit

35. Open Mind

36. Humour

Liberal MP for Preston in 1929, when he defected to join the Labour government as Attorney General. Jowitt perhaps never realised that Anrep had incorporated a joke at his expense. He professed himself delighted with his portrait, writing to the then Director of the National Gallery, Sir Philip Hendy, on 31 March 1951 that,

37. Leisure

'apart from its aesthetic qualities it is a very good likeness, and it may be useful for you when you are more particularly annoyed with me to have my face available so that you may stamp upon it'.[37]

Humour is celebrated as a *Modern Virtue* in a design which shows the society beauty Lady Diana Cooper dressed as Britannia with a copy of *Who's Who* under her arm, conferring a crown on Punch (fig. 36). Indeed, Humour appears at the top of Anrep's list of possible virtues in a hand-written note and on the back of a pencil plan for the floor dated 1945.[38] Punch is depicted as he appeared on the cover of *Punch* magazine in 1856. The editor professed his staff touched to see him so immortalised.[39]

One of the most imaginative designs is for Leisure (fig. 37). Anrep had originally planned to show a couple on the seashore, but the final mosaic shows the poet T.S. Eliot reclining on a balustrade in front of Loch Ness, contemplating Einstein's theory of relativity ($E=MC^2$). Before him on the terrace are a post-regency-style lounger and pieces of contemporary art and sculpture. To the right are two girls, one of whom bathes in the loch, with the monster in the distance. Anrep intended the mosaic to reflect 'the exceptional intellectuality of the poet and his poetic fantasy'.[40] The arts also feature in other images. In Delectation the celebrated ballerina Margot Fonteyn is depicted listening to the writer the Hon. Edward Sackville-West, a talented musician, playing the harpischord (fig. 38). Lewis Carroll's Alice appears in Wonder, where she encounters Augustus John in the guise of Neptune and a mermaid figurehead inviting her to embark on new adventures (fig. 39).

38. Delectation

39. Wonder

The arts and politics are combined in Compromise, which features one of Anrep's favourite film stars, the American actress Loretta Young (fig. 40). A frequent visitor to Britain, here she pours red and white wine into a loving cup, symbolising British and American friendship. She wears both a crown, symbolising royal government, and a Phrygian cap, an emblem of democracy. In the background is a symbolic bridge. Compromise only appeared on the list of virtues at a late stage, replacing Candour and Sincerity. However, for Anrep

40. Compromise

Compromise summed up the English character, as he told his Russian radio audience: 'In their political doings the English invariably hope to reach agreement on both sides. That is their national trait.'

Some of the figures in the mosaic were drawn from life, others from photographs. Sixth Sense (fig. 41) features the poet Edith Sitwell, who wrote to Anrep on 8 August 1946, 'I need not say that it will be the *greatest* pleasure to me to figure as the poet in your new mosaics. May I take this opportunity of saying in what great admiration I regard the earlier ones? The Cecil Beaton photographs of me are by far the best photographs that have been done, and I would much rather you used those than any other (fig. 42).'[41] Not everyone was asked in advance whether they would mind being

42. Cecil Beaton, 1904–1980
*Edith Sitwell*, 1927

41. Sixth Sense

included. T.S. Eliot, writing to Anrep on 17 November 1952 (after the completion of the floor) declared himself 'most flattered and interested to hear that I am included in your mosaic'.[42] Once sketches were complete, they were translated into mosaic. First a full-scale colour cartoon was made. Usually the stones were applied directly to this cartoon, so few survive. A rare example is the colour cartoon for the portrait of Earl Jowitt, where the position of every stone is outlined in pencil (fig. 43). As Maud Russell wrote to Graham Reynolds, Keeper at the Victoria and Albert Museum where the cartoon is preserved: 'Normally when Mr Anrep was doing portraits… there were no duplicates as he worked on the cartoon head himself and so it disappeared under the stones. Why this one was duplicated I don't know. All the other cartoon portraits have been covered and only sketches – small sketches – remain.'[43]

43. *Cartoon for Rt. Hon. Earl Jowitt*, about 1952
Pencil and Gouache on card, 42.5 x 31.2 cm
The Victoria and Albert Museum, London

Although, as Anrep said in his Russian radio broadcast, the floor is 'dedicated to the traits of the English character', it also includes a tribute to the Russian people and Anna Akhmatova. In his original description of the subjects for the Mosaics committee Anrep had proposed illustrating Warmth with a girl out camping, warming the dying leaves of a young tree with her breath, the Oxford skyline in the background. In the end, however, this became Compassion (fig. 44), which he described as follows on Russian radio: 'A Young woman is being saved from the deathly horrors of war by an angel. The bones of martyrs are thrown into a mass grave, as recorded in the documents of German concentration camps. It is not a portrait, but a memory of Anna Akhmatova in her youth and the siege of Leningrad.'

In her poetry Akhmatova had recorded with compassion the suffering of the Russian people through the Revolution, Stalin's Terror and the Second World War. Anrep felt deeply the contrast between her resolution to remain in Russia and share the fate of her compatriots and his own status as an *émigré*. In *Pominanie* (Commemoration), a group of five poems dedicated to Akhmatova written shortly before his death in 1969, Anrep recalled their last meeting in February 1917, during

44. Compassion

the early days of the Revolution, when he had tried to persuade her to flee. His voice alternates with hers.

> I visited you without my epaulettes,
> And at [your] feet begged you to flee.
> > 'What for? It's warmer lying in the grave
> > In one's fatherland. I mean – for me it is.'

> Her hand grips the roses tightly,
> And pain beats in my breast.
> We are alone…
> > 'now you must go,
> > I shall face the day of danger fearlessly.'

Anrep never told the National Gallery that he had included Akhmatova in the mosaic, perhaps thinking that the subject would not be of interest. It was only after his death that she was identified. Although Anrep linked the scene with the Siege of Leningrad (1941–3), the artist's daughter-in-law, Annabel Farjeon, believed that Anrep also meant the image to publicise the monstrosities perpetrated by the Russian government during this period, highlighting the fact that mass exterminations carried out under Stalin had killed even greater numbers of people than those murdered in Nazi concentration camps.[44] Anrep would have been unable to make this connection explicit in a 1950s broadcast for Communist Russia.

It was also after Anrep's death that Maud Russell revealed that she herself was the model for Folly (fig. 45). In a letter concerning fundraising for the Tate Gallery mosaics, Anrep had expressed his belief that it was counter to human nature to give money for such projects. 'I am a pessimist in general about the rich species of the human breed and therefore I consider it will be a miracle if you will squeeze a penny out of them', he wrote to the Keeper of the Tate Gallery, Charles Aitken, on 7 May 1922.[45] Nevertheless, it would still seem strange to include a patron as the personification of Folly, were it not for the fact that Russell and Anrep were secretly lovers from the 1940s. The portrait was, as she wrote, 'a whimsical joke'.[46] It shows Anrep's favourite view of her, full-face to show off her symmetrical features.[47] It refers perhaps in equal part to his folly for her as well as her 'folly' in supporting him.

During Anrep's lifetime Russell was shy about being associated with the mosaics. When in November 1950 Sir Philip Hendy suggested that an inscription recording her generosity should be incorporated into the design, she at first thought this a 'delightful idea', and it was agreed that her name would be included with the words *Maud Russell donavit, Anrep fecit.*[48] But she later had second thoughts and on 23 November 1952 she wrote to Hendy to ask that she remain anonymous.[49] The inscription remains in place in the West border of the mosaic.

Russell assisted with practical arrangements for the floor, updating the Gallery with progress reports, and assisting with paperwork concerning the import of the mosaic from France. She also played an important role in the development of ideas for the mosaics. She records in her diary how Anrep would regularly talk to her about his ideas. In her diary entry for 10 August 1945, she wrote, 'B worked on the arrangement of the panels for the NG floor. I had a great table found for him and placed in the window and there he works. I stood over him, we discussed the panel arrangement and how geometrical the floor should be and he made alterations and one improvement after another.' She records that he first had the idea for the Virtues while they were lunching at the 'Shanghai' on 19 August 1944. 'Boris said first the Seven Ages of Man presented of course in a modern manner. But this didn't appeal so much to him and he jumped on at once to the Seven Virtues and Vices and began exploring the possibilities and making suggestions. The Virtues should be treated rather paradoxically and cynically. They might be the old ones treated in those ways, or they might be a new set. And the same with the seven deadly sins. B began suggesting. I was to think and suggest. Friends were to suggest. The idea amused him.'

45. Folly

In her diary Russell also comments on how personal the choice of Virtues was for Anrep. In her entry for 12 May 1945 she records, 'I suggested dropping the name "Virtues"….[it] raised the wrong sort of anticipation in everyone he talked to about them. Nor indeed was his choice noble enough to merit the name. Humour, Ease, Invention, Warmth, Imperfection, Argument, Relativity, Appetite or Relish, Non-Conformity, Hazard, Sixth Sense, Quest, Wonder and Imagination were at one time or the other on the list. "Human Qualities" would be better than "Virtues".'

46. Here I Lie

47. Rest and be Thankful

Apart from the Virtues, the floor also includes a picture of the tomb of the artist (with his profile, his hammer and trowel and the inscription 'Here I lie') and a picture of a Kent pub sign 'Rest and be thankful' (figs 46 and 47). Vulliamy wrote: 'The tools on his notional gravestone indicated I think that in another world quite free from all earthly tracasseries, Boris wished to be sitting, hammer in hand before a heap of small stones... Yet, there is no better, more poetical memorial to him in that splendid pavement, than the colours of the fallen leaves of the autumnal *marroniers*, the chestnut trees so symbolic of the Boulevard Arago.'[50]

Following his completion of the National Gallery mosaics, Anrep continued to work tirelessly until well into his seventies, creating mosaics for St Anne's Chapel in Mullingar Cathedral in Ireland (1954), further mosaics for the Bank of England (1957), and an important cycle for the Chapel of the Blessed Sacrament in Westminster Cathedral (1962). This was to be his last great work. Maroussia had died in 1956, and in 1965 Helen died. That year Anrep met Akhmatova for the last time in Paris, shortly before her death. The meeting upset Anrep because he could not show Akhmatova the ring that she had given him when he was in Russia. It had been stolen from his Hampstead studio following an air raid in 1944. He and Maud Russell (fig. 48) continued to be close, living in adjoining flats at 2 and 4, No. 6 Hyde Park Gardens. He died on 7 June 1969 and was buried at Mottisfont Abbey.

48. Maud Russell and Boris Anrep

# NOTES

1  Anrep, English radio broadcast

2  Gathorne-Hardy ed., 1963, p. 211

3  ibid., p. 204

4  Baron, p. 120

5  Anrep, Letter to Alexander Samuelovich, 1 July 1968, National Art Library MSL/1973/1324/218. For Akhmatova's feelings about Anrep see Haight and Rosslyn.

6  Gathorne-Hardy ed., 1974, p. 98

7  Spalding, pp. 247–9. The quotation about collages comes from Partridge, *A Pacifist's War*, 1978, p. 201

8  Vulliamy, p. 13

9  Holroyd, 1996, p. 315

10  Partridge, MSL/1974/16160. Anrep bought a cake of this type to Lytton Strachey's house for Christmas 1924 (Holroyd, 1994, p. 541)

11  National Art Library MSL/1973/1324/10

12  Partridge, MSL/1974/16160

13  London 1913, p. 9

14  Baron, p. 120

15  Fry, pp. 227–78

16  London 1973, p. 1

17  Henderson, National Art Library MSL/1974/16160

18  Vulliamy, pp. 9–10 and 16–17

19  ibid., p. 21

20  London, 1973, p. 1

21  Russell, Diary, 5 March 1943

22  Both letters in the National Art Library 86NN11

23  MacColl, p. 128

24  Whittick, p. 79

25  *Evening News*, 4 November 1929.

26  Letters between Anrep and Holmes in National Gallery Archive

27  Furst, *Apollo*, p. 161

28  *The Times*, 1 June 1928

29  Letters dated 10 January 1927 and 27 July 1926 in National Art Library 86NN11; copies in National Gallery Archive

30  Anrep, Russian radio broadcast

31  National Art Library 86NN11

32  National Gallery Archive

33  Letter dated 1 November, National Art Library 86NN11

34  Letter to Martin Davies, 8 December 1970, National Gallery Archive

35  Anrep, English radio broadcast

36  Anrep, description of subjects submitted to Mosaics committee at an early stage, National Gallery Archive

37  National Gallery Archive

38  National Art Library MSL/1973/1324/101 and Victoria and Albert Museum E. 14-1983

39  National Art Library MSL/1973/1324/121

40  Anrep, Russian radio broadcast

41  National Art Library MSL/1973/1324/38

42  National Art Library MSL/1973/1324/108

43  Letter dated February 1970, Victoria and Albert Museum Archive

44  Farjeon 2003, pp. 160–1 (page reference is to unpublished English manuscript)

45  Tate Archive

46  Letter to Martin Davies, 8 December 1970, National Gallery Archive

47  Russell, Diary, 2 April 1943

48  Philip Hendy, letter to Maud Russell, 27 November 1950, National Art Library 86NN11, and Maud Russell, letter to Philip Hendy, 3 December 1950, National Gallery Archive

49  National Gallery Archive

50  Vulliamy, p. 34

'Mining' from *The Labours of Life*, 1928

# THE LIFE OF BORIS ANREP

| | |
|---|---|
| 1883 | 28 September, Boris Anrep is born in St Petersburg. |
| 1899 | Anrep spends the summer learning English in Great Missenden, Buckinghamshire. |
| 1902–05 | Anrep studies law in St Petersburg. |
| 1905 | Anrep meets Yuniya Kitrovo and they begin an affair. |
| 1908 | Anrep marries Yuniya and the couple move to Paris, where Anrep enrolls at the Académie Julian. |
| 1910 | Anrep and Yuniya spend the winter of 1910–11 in Edinburgh where Anrep studies drawing and starts to mix in British artistic circles. |
| 1911 | Helen Maitland becomes Anrep's mistress; Anrep, Yuniya and Helen divide their time between Paris and London. |
| 1912 | Anrep selects the Russian exhibits for the Second Post-Impressionist Exhibition. |
| | In December Helen gives birth to a daughter, Anastasia. |
| 1914 | In July Helen gives birth to a son, Igor. Yuniya returns to Russia. |
| 1914–16 | Anrep serves as a member of the Russian Imperial Guard in Galicia and begins a relationship with Anna Akhmatova. |
| 1917 | Anrep is called back to England as Military Secretary to the Russian Government committee. He brings with him Mariya Volkova (Maroussia) who becomes his mistress. He visits Russia for the last time in September 1917. |
| 1918 | Anrep and Yuniya divorce, and on 17 April Anrep marries Helen. He invites Maroussia to live with them at 4 Pond Street, Hampstead. |
| 1926 | Helen leaves Anrep for Roger Fry. Anrep moves to Paris with Maroussia, and sets up a studio at 65 Boulevard Arago, Paris. |
| 1930 | Jeanne Reynal becomes Anrep's mistress and assistant. Their affair lasts until 1938. |
| 1940 | Anrep and Maroussia escape from Paris before the German occupation and return to London, setting up home at Heath Studio, North End, Hampstead. He meets Maud Russell. |
| 1941–43 | Anrep works nights as a monitor for Reuters, transcribing Russian broadcasts. |
| 1945 | After the war Anrep returns to Paris with Maroussia. |
| 1956 | Death of Maroussia. |
| 1965 | Anrep gives up the Paris studio and goes to live with Maud Russell at 6 Hyde Park Gardens. Death of Helen Anrep. |
| 1966 | Death of Anna Akhmatova. |
| 1969 | 7 June, Boris Anrep dies and is buried at Mottisfont Abbey. |

# THE WORKS OF BORIS ANREP

| | |
|---|---|
| 1913 | A selection of Anrep's drawings, paintings and mosaics is exhibited at the Chenil Gallery, Chelsea, together with embroideries designed by Anrep and executed by Yuniya. |
| 1914 | Mosaic for the Crypt in Westminster Cathedral. |
| 1917 | Mosaic floor for Miss Ethel Sands at 15 The Vale, Chelsea. |
| 1919 | Mosaic for Augustus John at Mallord Street, Chelsea (now in the Victoria and Albert Museum). |
| 1920 | Mosaic wall decorations for Miss Ethel Sands at 15 The Vale, Chelsea. |
| 1921 | *The Vision of St John* for the apse of the Memorial Chapel in the Church of the Royal Military College, Sandhurst. Fireplace for Lytton Strachey's bedroom at Ham Spray (now at Rodwell House, Baylham, Suffolk). |
| 1922 | Mosaic floor, *Daily Incidents in the Life of a Lady of Fashion*, for William and Lesley Jowitt at 35 Upper Brook Street, Mayfair (now in Birmingham City Art Gallery). |
| 1923 | Mosaic floor for the Blake Room in the Tate Gallery at Millbank, illustrating 'The Proverbs of Hell' from *The Marriage of Heaven and Hell* by William Blake. |
| 1924 | *The Blessed Oliver Plunkett* for Westminster Cathedral. |
| 1925 | Mosaic of angels raising the figure of Christ for the apse of General Stirling's private chapel in Keir House at Dunblane, Perthshire. |
| 1927–46 | Mosaics for the Bank of England at Threadneedle Street. |
| 1928 | *The Labours of Life* for the National Gallery. Mosaic for the Greek Orthodox Church of St Sophia, Moscow Road, Bayswater. |
| 1929 | *The Pleasures of Life* for the National Gallery. |
| 1933 | *The Awakening of the Muses* for the National Gallery. Mantelpiece for Ralph and Frances Partridge at Ham Spray (now at 3 Linden Park Road, Tunbridge Wells). |
| c. 1938 | Mosaic decoration for a gazebo for Lord Moyne at Biddesdon, with three muses in alcoves. |
| 1945 | *Sacred Heart* mosaic for Mrs Stirling (left by her to Ampleforth in 1972). *The Trinity* mosaic for Maud Russell's home at Mottisfont Abbey. |
| 1947 | Mosaic portrait of Maud Russell as the angel of Mottisfont, for the outer wall of the Chapter House, Mottisfont Abbey. |
| 1949 | *St Patrick Lighting the Fire at Slane* for St Patrick's Chapel in Mullingar Cathedral, Ireland. |
| 1952 | *The Modern Virtues* for the National Gallery. Second mosaic for the Greek Orthodox Church of St Sophia, Moscow Road, Bayswater. |
| 1953 | Memorial plaques for the tomb of Greek ship-owner Kulukundis, Hendon Vale Cemetery. |
| 1954 | Mosaic decoration for St Anne's Chapel in Mullingar Cathedral, Ireland. Third mosaic for the Greek Orthodox Church of St Sophia, Moscow Road, Bayswater. |
| 1955 | Mosaic for the altar in Notre Dame de France, Leicester Place, London (covered with a fresco by Jean Cocteau in 1959). |
| 1957 | Mosaics for the Bank of England at New Change. |
| 1962 | Chapel of the Blessed Sacrament, Westminster Cathedral. Fireplace for Frances Partridge at Halkin Street, London. |
| 1965 | Tabletop for Igor and Annabel Anrep. |

'Rest' from *The Pleasures of Life*, 1929

# BIBLIOGRAPHY

Boris Anrep, 'Foreword to the Book of Anrep', *Poetry and Drama*, September 1913, pp. 275–90

Boris Anrep, English radio broadcast, National Art Library manuscript MSL/1973/1324/55

Boris Anrep, Russian radio broadcast, National Art Library manuscript MSL/1973/1324/56

Boris Anrep, unpublished correspondence and papers in the National Gallery Archive, National Art Library and Tate Archive

Boris Anrep, 'Mosaics', *Journal of the RIBA*, vol. 34, third series, no. 6, 22 January 1927

Wendy Baron, *Miss Ethel Sands and her Circle*, London 1977

J.R. Bullen, 'Byzantinism and Modernism 1900–14', *Burlington Magazine*, November 1999

Annabel Farjeon, 'Mosaics and Boris Anrep', *Charleston Magazine*, no. 7, 1993, pp. 15–22

Annabel Farjeon, 'Anna Akhmatova and Boris Anrep', *Charleston Magazine*, no. 10, 1994, pp. 20–4

Annabel Farjeon, 'The Adventures of a Russian Artist: A Biography of Boris Anrep', *The Star Magazine*, St Petersburg 2003 (unpublished English manuscript kindly lent by the Boris Anrep Family Estate)

Roger Fry, 'Modern Mosaic and Mr Boris Anrep', *The Burlington Magazine*, vol. 42, no. 243, 1923, pp. 272–8

Herbert Furst, 'Boris Anrep and his Mosaics', *Artwork*, 1929, pp. 22–33

Herbert Furst, 'The Boris Anrep Pavement in the National Gallery', *Apollo*, 9, 1929, pp. 158–61

R. Gathorne-Hardy ed., *Ottoline. The Early Memoirs of Lady Ottoline Morrell*, London 1963

R. Gathorne-Hardy ed., *Ottoline at Garsington, Memoirs of Lady Ottoline Morrell 1915–18*, London 1974

Amanda Haight, *Anna Akhmatova: A Poetic Pilgrimage*, Oxford 1976

Nicholas Henderson, 'Boris Anrep', National Art Library manuscript MSL/1974/16160

Michael Holroyd, *Lytton Strachey*, London 1994

Michael Holroyd, *Augustus John*, London 1996

Catriona Kelly, 'Anna Akhmatova and Boris Anrep: an afterword', *Irish Slavonic Studies*, 16, 1995, pp. 1–29

London 1912, *Second Post-Impressionist Exhibition*, Grafton Galleries, London 1912

London 1913, *Boris Anrep*, Chenil Gallery, London 1913

London 1973, *Boris Anrep* (1883–1969): A Loan Exhibition, Edward Harvane Gallery, London 1973

London 1974, *Henry Lamb and his friends (Boris Anrep, Stanley Spencer, Augustus John, Gilbert Spencer)*, Edward Harvane Gallery, London 1974

René MacColl, 'Modern Life in Mosaic: Boris Anrep at the National Gallery', *The Studio*, February 1930, pp. 128–9

Angelina Morhange, *Boris Anrep: The National Gallery Mosaics*, London 1979

Frances Partridge, 'Boris Anrep', National Art Library manuscript MSL/1974/16160

Frances Partridge, *A Pacifist's War*, London 1978

Wendy Rosslyn, 'Boris Anrep and the poems of Anna Akhmatova', *Modern Language Review*, vol. 74, no. 4, October 1979, pp. 884–96

Maud Russell, 'Diary Excerpts and reminiscences relating to Boris Anrep', National Art Library manuscript 86NN63

Maud Russell, Correspondence and Papers concerning Boris Anrep, National Art Library manuscripts 86NN61, 86W75

Frances Spalding, *Roger Fry*, London 1980

Justin Vulliamy, 'Ars Musivariae', February 1971, National Art Library manuscript MSL/1974/16161

Arnold Whittick, 'The Art of Mosaic and the work of Mr Boris Anrep', *Masterbuilder*, March 1935, pp. 72–9

# NORTH VESTIBULE: *THE MODERN VIRTUES* (opened 25 November 1952)

1  COMPASSION

The Russian poet Anna Akhmatova (1889–1966) is shown escaping from the horrors of war. On the right is a mass grave of victims of the Siege of Leningrad (1941–43). Akhmatova shared and gave expression to the suffering of the Russian people through the Revolution, the Stalinist Terror and the Second World War. She was persecuted by successive Soviet regimes, and between 1925–40 and 1946–50 was banned from writing.

2  COMPROMISE

The American actress Loretta Young (1913–2000) fills a loving cup with red and white wine, symbolising British and American friendship. The bridge behind her symbolises the bond of friendship between the two countries. She wears both a crown, symbolising royal government, and a Phrygian republican cap, symbolic of democracy.

3  CURIOSITY

A bust of the eminent physicist Lord Rutherford (1871–1937) stands next to the primitive apparatus that he used to split the atom in 1932. A pioneer of modern atomic science, Lord Rutherford had been awarded the Nobel Prize in 1908. He discovered alpha, beta and gamma rays and had been the first to recognise the nuclear nature of the atom in 1911.

4  DELECTATION

The ballerina Margot Fonteyn (1919–1991) listens to the Hon. Edward Sackville-West playing the harpsichord, with a statue of the Roman goddess Pomona in the background. Fonteyn created many roles for Frederick Ashton's ballets and formed a legendary partnership with Rudolf Nureyev. Edward Sackville-West made his career as a writer, but was also a talented keyboard player. He encouraged many younger musicians and took an active interest in the development of Covent Garden Opera.

5  DEFIANCE

The British Prime Minister Winston Churchill (1874–1965) stands before the white cliffs of Dover wearing his wartime siren suit and making his famous victory sign in defiance of a swastika-shaped monster threatening Britain's shores. The monster wears a pope's crown, presumably an indirect reference to Italy, one of the Axis powers.

6  FOLLY

The society hostess and patron of the arts, Mrs Maud Russell (1891–1982) is shown with a jester's puppet. She was a close friend of Anrep and it was she who paid for *The Modern Virtues*.

# BORIS ANREP'S NATIONAL GALLERY MOSAICS

Boris Anrep's four colourful mosaics decorate the three vestibules and the half-way landing of the imposing staircase built by Sir John Taylor in 1887 for the entrance hall of the National Gallery. The first mosaic was completed in 1928, the last in 1952.

All the mosaics were paid for by private patrons. Samuel Courtauld, the industrialist who twice served as Chairman of the Trustees of the National Gallery, and Anrep's friend Maud Russell, wife of the banker Gilbert Russell, were the main benefactors.

Anrep (1885–1969) was born in Russia, and educated in England and at St Petersburg University. He then travelled extensively to study mosaics in his own country, the Near East and Italy, and attended the Académie Julian in Paris and the Edinburgh College of Art. Around this time he became friends with the painters Augustus John and Henry Lamb. In 1912 Anrep worked alongside the art critic Clive Bell on Roger Fry's important Post-Impressionist exhibition which was shown in London. Both Augustus John and Clive Bell were to feature in the National Gallery mosaics. Later Anrep met the economist Maynard Keynes, a great admirer of the Bloomsbury Group whose members included the writers Virginia Woolf and Lytton Strachey as well as Bell and Fry. Keynes' wife, the dancer Lydia Lopokova, and Virginia Woolf also feature in the mosaics.

In 1926, three years after completing the mosaic floor of the Blake Room in the Tate Gallery, Anrep began work on the National Gallery commission. The subject, which Anrep described as a philosophical cycle, is based on the intellectual life of the 'modern' age – the mid-1920s to the mid-1950s. *The Labours of Life* in the west vestibule illustrates Man's constructive and creative nature and includes such subjects as a workman with an electric drill and a sculptor modelling a statue. On the opposite vestibule floor is *The Pleasures of Life* showing Man's recreations. There are scenes of sporting and other relaxing pastimes.

Both *Labours* and *Pleasures* are linked in subject to Apollo and Bacchus in the third mosaic, *The Awakening of the Muses*, which was completed in 1933 on the half-way landing. Here the figures are portraits of well-known contemporaries. Sir Osbert Sitwell, man of letters and champion of the new movements in art, is represented as Apollo, who usually stands for the rational and civilised side of Man's nature. Alongside is a portrait of Clive Bell as Bacchus, representing the pleasurable side of life. They are surrounded by the Muses, the nine goddesses of creative inspiration, each of whom had her own sphere of influence over Learning and the Arts. We find Virginia Woolf portrayed as Clio, the Muse of History; Lydia Lopokova, the prima ballerina, as Terpsichore, the Muse of Dancing; the film star Greta Garbo as Melpomene, the Muse of Tragedy; and the Countess Jowitt, whom Anrep had already portrayed in 1922 in his mosaic floor *Various Moments in the Day of a Lady of Fashion* (now in Birmingham Museum and Art Gallery) is shown as Thalia, the Muse of Comedy.

# THE MOSAICS

## NORTH VESTIBULE
### THE MODERN VIRTUES

17 FOLLY Mrs Gilbert Russell, patron of the Arts.

18 HUMOUR Lady Diana Cooper as Britannia crowns Punch, the embodiment of Humour.

19 LEISURE The poet T.S. Eliot contemplates Loch Ness and Einstein's formula; symbols of Painting and Sculpture are on the left.

20 LUCIDITY The philosopher Bertrand Russell pulls the symbolic figure of Truth from a well and plucks off her mask.

21 OPEN MIND The Rt Hon Earl Jowitt, in his robes as Lord Chancellor, in front of statues of Hecate and Justice.

22 PURSUIT The astronomer Professor Sir Fred Hoyle is represented as a steeplejack.

23 SIXTH SENSE The writer Dame Edith Sitwell, reading a book of poems, crosses a chasm unafraid, while terrifying beasts and a raven threaten.

24 WONDER The painter Augustus John as Neptune offers Alice in Wonderland gifts from the sea, while a figurehead invites her to embark on new adventures.

25 HERE I LIE The tomb of Boris Anrep emblazoned with a self-portrait relief, a hammer and trowel and a family crest.

26 REST AND BE THANKFUL The signboard of a public house in Kent.

Opened 25 November 1952, the gift of Mrs Gilbert Russell.

## EAST VESTIBULE
### THE PLEASURES OF LIFE

ssan poet Anna
e horrors of war.

nerican actress Loretta
(Phrygian) cap as
wing cup with red and

the physicist Lord
ing atom.

Churchill stands
f Dover and defies an
e shape of a swastika.
shores.

allerina Dame Margot
ton. Edward Sackville-
chord.

# PLAN OF TH[E

## HALF-WAY LANDING
### THE AWAKENING OF THE MUSES

1  POLYHYMNIA Muse of Heroic Hymns
   Hon. Mrs Bryan Guinness (Diana Mitford).

2  EUTERPE Muse of Music
   Christabel. Lady Aberconway.

3  ERATO Muse of Lyric Poetry
   Mrs St John Hutchinson.

4  BACCHUS God of Wine
   Clive Bell.

5  APOLLO God of Music
   Sir Osbert Sitwell.

6  CLIO Muse of History
   Virginia Woolf.

7  THALIA Muse of Comedy
   The Countess Jowitt.

8  CALLIOPE Muse of Epic Poetry
   Unknown Sitter.

9  URANIA Muse of Astronomy
   Madame Maria Volkova. Anrep's sister-in-law.

10 MELPOMENE Muse of Tragedy
   Greta Garbo.

11 TERPSICHORE Muse of Dancing
   Lady Keynes (Lydia Lopokova).

Opened July 1933. the gift of Samuel Courtauld
and other benefactors.

12 COMPASSION The Ru[
   Akhmatova. surrounded
   is visited by an angel.

13 COMPROMISE The A[
   Young, wearing a Libert[
   well as a crown. fills a
   white wine.

14 CURIOSITY A bust of
   Rutherford. with a split

15 DEFIANCE Sir Winsto[
   before the white cliffs
   apocalyptic beast. in th[
   which threatens British

16 DELECTATION The b[
   Fonteyn listens to the
   West playing the harps[

WEST VESTIBULE

# An Introduction to
# BORIS ANREP'S MOSAICS

## at the
# NATIONAL GALLERY
# LONDON

During this same period Anrep was also working on mosaic floors in the Bank of England (1927–42). World War II intervened and in 1945 the Trustees agreed to the commission for the north vestibule, the fourth and final mosaic in the series. This was perhaps Anrep's most important work of the 1950s, completed before his mosaics in the Chapel of the Blessed Sacrament in Westminster Cathedral which were laid between 1956 and 1962.

Modern Virtues is a record of the intellectual life of the 1930s and 1940s: famous contemporaries are used to represent the Virtues and refer to the Arts, the Sciences, Philosophy, Politics and Law. The poet Anna Akhmatova, whom Anrep had known as a student in Russia, is featured as 'Compassion'; the American film actress Loretta Young, who won an Oscar in 1947, is 'Compromise'; 'Curiosity' is Lord Rutherford, developer of the nuclear theory of the atom; and in the centre is Sir Winston Churchill, Prime Minister of the United Kingdom (1940–5 and 1951–5), as 'Defiance'. Dame Margot Fonteyn, prima ballerina assoluta, appears in 'Delectation'; the poet and playwright T.S. Eliot, winner of the Nobel Prize for Literature in 1948, features in 'Leisure'; Bertrand Russell, the philosopher, winner of the Nobel Prize for Literature in 1950, illustrates 'Lucidity'; Professor Sir Fred Hoyle, the astronomer, Dame Edith Sitwell, poet and critic, and Augustus John are portrayed respectively in 'Pursuit', 'Sixth Sense' and 'Wonder'.

'Floor mosaics can be approached from different angles and a particularly intimate relationship is created between them and the onlooker', Anrep wrote. He believed that floors were particularly suitable for pictorial decoration and that treading on the representations creates a sensual pleasure absent when a spectator views a picture hanging on a wall. Mosaic can also introduce colour into buildings.

Rather than use the 'in situ' method of laying mosaic, Anrep adopted the indirect transfer method, which allowed much of the work to be done in the studio. Cartoons were drawn to scale and traced onto strong paper which became a backing for the individually chipped pieces of marble and coloured glass, the tesserae. Anrep may have obtained these from Venice. Each tessera was glued separately onto the tracing to form the whole composition in reverse. The sheets of the glued tesserae were then laid paper upwards onto the prepared concrete floor. Water was then applied to the paper so that it could be peeled off. Finally the mosaic was treated with a marble polishing machine.

Anrep was one of the first mosaicists of modern times to design his own cartoons as well as to execute them and the National Gallery works are amongst the most important that he laid.

A plan of the mosaics is shown overleaf.

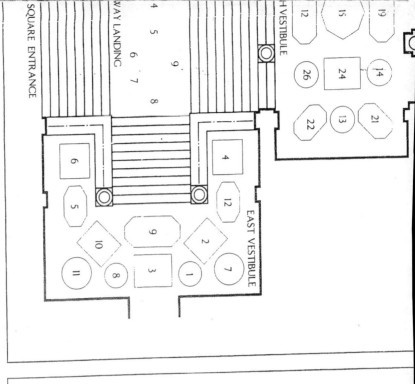

1 CHRISTMAS PUDDING A pudding aflame with brandy.

2 CONTEMPLATION Three men in thought.

3 CONVERSATION Two girls talking in front of a fireplace.

4 CRICKET A batsman about to be caught at the wicket.

5 DANCE A girl jiving.

6 FOOTBALL Two footballers tackling.

7 HUNTING A huntsman with his horse and dogs.

8 MUD PIE Three mud pies, a bucket and spade.

9 PROFANE LOVE A man and two girls, one with a dog.

10 REST A girl in a hammock; another reading a newspaper on the grass.

11 SEA-HORSE A girl riding an inflatable horse.

12 SPEED A girl riding the pillion of a motorcycle.

Opened 13 November 1929, the gift of Samuel Courtauld and other benefactors.

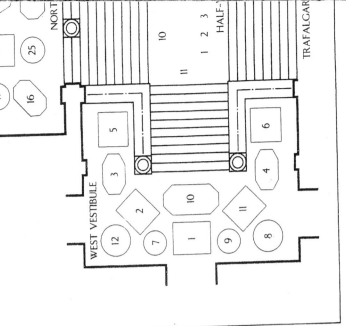

WEST VESTIBULE

NORT...

TRAFALGAR

HALF-...

1  2  3

10

11

## THE LABOURS OF LIFE

1 ART  A sculptor modelling a statue.

2 ASTRONOMY  An astronomer at his telescope.

3 COMMERCE  A Covent Garden porter carrying a pile of baskets.

4 ENGINEERING  A man working an electric drill.

5 EXPLORING  A man taking a moving picture of a zebra.

6 FARMING  A woman washing a pig.

7 LETTERS  A still life of a child's slate and sponge with the names of favourite children's books.

8 MINING  A coalminer at work.

9 MUSIC  A still life of a shell, a flute and a book.

10 SACRED LOVE  A father, mother, child and dog.

11 SCIENCE  A student of prehistoric animals in the Natural History Museum.

12 THEATRE  A contortionist.

Opened 31 May 1928, the gift of Samuel Courtauld and other benefactors.

ISBN 1-85709-023-3

Code No. 525176

© National Gallery Publications Ltd 1993. Printed in Great Britain.

9 781857 090239 >